Coming to America

The Kids' Book About Immigration

David Fassler, M.D.
Kimberly Danforth, M.A.

Waterfront Books
86 Lake Street
Burlington, Vermont 05401

Distributed to the book trade by
The Talman Company
131 Spring Street, Suite 201 E-N
New York, NY 10012

Designed and produced by Robinson Book Associates
Printed in the United States by Daamen, Inc.

Library of Congress Cataloging in Publication Data

Fassler, David.
    Coming to America: the kids' book about immigration / David
Fassler, Kimberly Danforth.
        p.   cm.
    Summary: Children who have immigrated to the United States
describe their experiences in adjusting to a new country and culture.
Includes drawings made by the children.
    ISBN: 0-914525-23-9 (pbk.): $12.95 — ISBN 0-914525-24-7
(plastic, comb spiral binding): $16.95.
    1. Children of immigrants — United States — Juvenile literature.
2. United States – Emigration and immigration – Juvenile literature.
3. Children's drawings. [1. United States – Emigration and immigration.
2. Children's art.] I. Danforth, Kimberly, 1961-.
II. Title.
HQ792.U5F37   1992
304.8 — dc20   92-36478
                                                              CIP
                                                              AC

Introduction

Over 500,000 families immigrate to the United States each year. By the end of the decade, this number is expected to triple.

Immigrant children face many challenges: the struggle for acceptance, the difficulty of learning English, and the challenge of becoming bicultural in a society that generally promotes a single culture.

Many refugee children have traumatic pasts. Some have experienced war firsthand. Others may be fleeing desperate economic circumstances, religious or political persecution, or natural disasters. All have endured major disruptions in the stability and predictability of their lives. However, regardless of their circumstances, all children move through similar phases in the process of adjusting to a new country and culture.

Coming to America was written with the help of children between the ages of 5 and 12. Through their words and drawings, readers both learn about and recognize the thoughts, feelings, and questions they and other children have about their move to America. In reading this book, children will also realize that other children — even those who speak English as their first language — share similar experiences. The book is not designed to address all issues or questions children may have regarding immigration. However, used in a supportive context, *Coming to America* can help facilitate open and honest discussion about a child's immigration experience.

On Using This Book

Coming to America is designed to be used interactively. Kids can draw and write on its pages. Such creative expression helps them accept and feel enthusiastic about cultural differences. The drawings also help limited-English-speaking children to understand the narrative and provide an opportunity for discussion. Young readers of *Coming to America* often identify with the feelings that children reveal in this book through their words and pictures, stimulating feelings of acceptance and sharing within the child. Choose a quiet, private place in which to share this book. Teachers and caring adults may learn valuable information about a student's homeland, family experiences, and other perceptions that may be difficult for the child to recount.

Suggestions for Parents

- Explain to your child that this is a different kind of book, one in which he or she can share feelings and thoughts through both drawings and words. Unlike school books or library books, this is a book in which to write or draw.

- Make sure the child has access to writing and drawing materials.

- Let the child work on the book at his or her own pace and choose the order in which to complete the chapters. Children will use the book in many different ways.

- If you are reading the book with a child, pick a quiet time and a private place. This is a time to concentrate on the child and his or her feelings.

- Be accepting and nonjudgmental. Let the child know that there are no right or wrong answers. Accept the child's emotions as valid and important.

- When working through the sections on the child's homeland and departure circumstances, help the child understand the terms pertaining to his or her own family situation. This can be an opportunity to correct misunderstandings.

- When the child wants to stop working on the book, respect his or her wishes. You can always return to the book at a later time.

Suggestions for Classroom Teachers

Coming to America contributes to a classroom atmosphere that is accepting of and enthusiastic about cultural differences. Sensitivity and awareness are a teacher's greatest assets when working with new arrivals and limited-English-speaking students.

Children from other countries who are learning English are not deficient. Rather, they are a rich source of cultural and linguistic information. Usually, immigrants have a command of a language and a culture that neither the other students nor the teacher has. Review the first section, "Suggestions for Parents" to gain an understanding of the book's use.

- Children should not be graded or judged on the activities contained in the book.

- This book may elicit strong emotions from some children. Using the book may help you identify children who should be referred to the school guidance counselor.

Suggestions for English as a Second Language (ESL) Instructors

Coming to America can be used for teaching English as a second language. The wookbook functions well in multicultural classes—in small group tutorials or entire classrooms of learners. The discussions and drawings in this book provide cues for conversation, narrative, written passages, and journal work. They also reinforce vocabulary and grammar patterns of the new language.

For beginning ESL students:

- Provide the children with paper and crayons and pose a question from the book that ties in with their current work in grammar patterns, vocabulary, or subject. Set a time limit of somewhere between 5 and 20 minutes, then ask them to draw and label their pictures as you make suggestions, ask questions, and encourage individual students at their seats. At the end of the time limit, hang all pictures where everyone can see them. Do not post drawings of students who are hesitant to share their own work in front of the class. As a class, consider the drawings one by one, and ask for comments and observations.

For intermediate ESL students:

- Conduct the above activity, only ask students to write a brief passage about their drawing on the back or bottom of the same paper. Volunteers share the drawings and the accompanying passages with the whole class, followed by a question and answer period.

Additional Activities:

- The ESL classroom may publish its own book based on the questions and drawings elicited from *Coming to America*. Students select their own topics and act as editors in choosing a cover, title, and sequence. Non-immigrant students may be asked to contribute comments and drawings once the first edition is presented to the mainstream classroom.

- Using mime or total physical response (TPR) techniques, ESL students may enact a situation posed or revealed in *Coming to America*. Each student adopts a character of a teacher, parent, authority figure, favorite pet, native person, etc. A play or performance may be staged and/or filmed.

- Encourage students to share folk art, native clothing, songs, and games from their first countries.

- To reveal the cultural diversity of a classroom, ask where and how the students got their names.

- Encourage new arrivals to write or draw pictures to send to their grandparents, relatives, and friends in their native country.

Suggestions for Counselors and Therapists

- *Coming to America* may be used in the context of individual therapy to enhance the child's expression of his or her thoughts and feelings. Reading the book can also be supportive and reassuring as the child realizes that his or her experiences are similar to those of other immigrant children.

- *Coming to America* is a therapeutic tool that can be used in conjunction with other expressive techniques such as play, art, music, drama, and movement.

- Allow the child to work through the book at his or her own pace, paying particular attention to the sections most pertinent to the child's situation, experiences, and emotional needs.

- In a therapy group setting, provide opportunities for children to complete the drawing and writing activities suggested in the book. Drawings, stories, poems, and other creative expressions generated by the group can be shared and discussed. Copies can also be collated and distributed to group members.

Acknowledgments

We would like to thank the following friends and colleagues for their encouragement, contributions, and constructive feedback:

Susan Ayers, M.S.W.
Sue Blethen
Anna Cotton
Billy Cotton
Mary Cotton
Nancy Cotton, Ph.D.
Paula Duncan, M.D.
Ann Epstein, M.D.
Monica Hutt
Caroline Linse, Ed.D.
Jim McCobb
Sue Niquette
Toni Schlenoff

Dan Talbert
Kathy Talbert
Anna Towne
Nathan Towne
Nicholas Towne
Yuen Uen
Anne Watson
Heidi Western
Judith Wright
Rural Education Center
Sara Holbrook Center
Welcoming New Americans Committee

We are also grateful to the many children who shared their thoughts, feelings, questions, and creative expressions.

Coming to America

I do not want my house to be walled in on all sides and my windows to be stuffed. I want the cultures of all lands to be blown about my house as freely as possible. —Mahatma Gandhi

Some families live in the same place for a really long time.

They may live in the same country, the same town, or even the same house.

My grandpa built our house,

My mom went to the same school I go to.

I sleep in my dad's old room.

Other families move to different places. Sometimes families move close by. Other times they move far away.

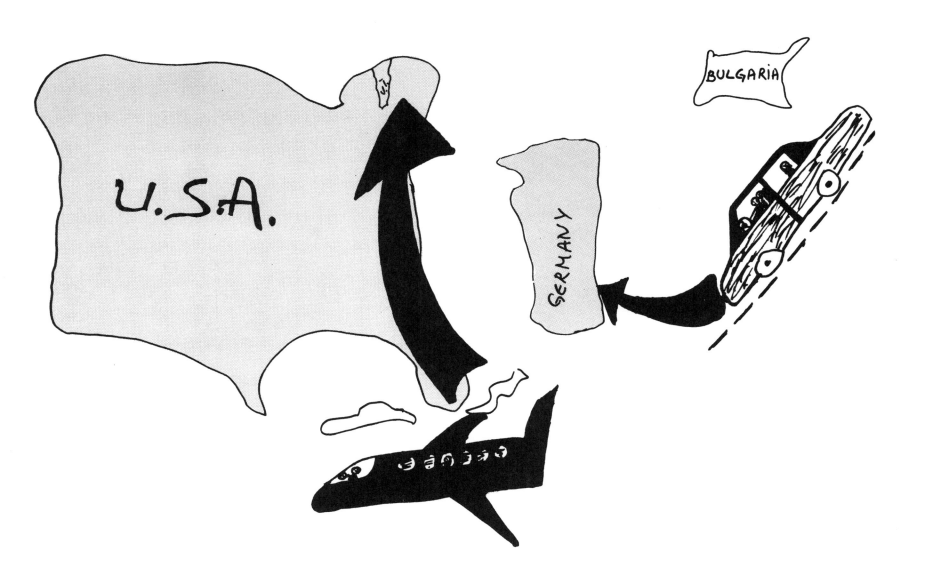

Some families move lots of times.

Sometimes families move slowly and carefully, packing up all their things.

My dad's in the Army. We have to move almost every year.

Other times, families have to move quickly. They may not have enough time to pack everything up. They may have to choose just a few important things to bring with them.

How did your family move? Did you have time to pack up all your things?

Draw a picture of you and your family getting ready to move.

Families move for different reasons.

My mom got a new job.

My parents got a divorce.

My dad went back to school.

We moved so I could have my own room!

My mom got remarried.

Every year, many families decide to come to America. They come to America for lots of different reasons.

There wasn't enough food where we used to live.

23

We came here to be with my grandma because she's old and she needed us to help her.

We moved so no one would bother us when we went to church.

We came to america
So my dad could
Work with his brother

Why did your family come to America?

Some families came to America because people were fighting where they used to live.

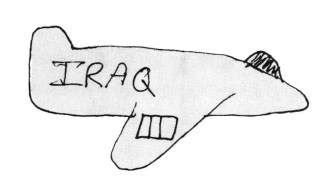

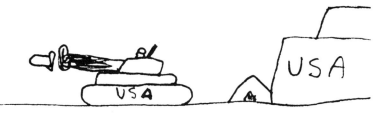

There were tanks in the street ouside our house. I was scared.

We lived in Ireland. My cousin got hurt when a bomb blew up near his school. That's why we moved.

I used to live in Lebanon. Everybody was fighting all the time. With guns and stuff. So we moved here to be safe.

The police were putting everybody in jail.

Was there any fighting where you used to live?

Draw a picture of what you saw or heard.

Families come to America from all over the world.

I came from Guatemala.

I used to live in Israel.

I was born in China.

We used to live in France

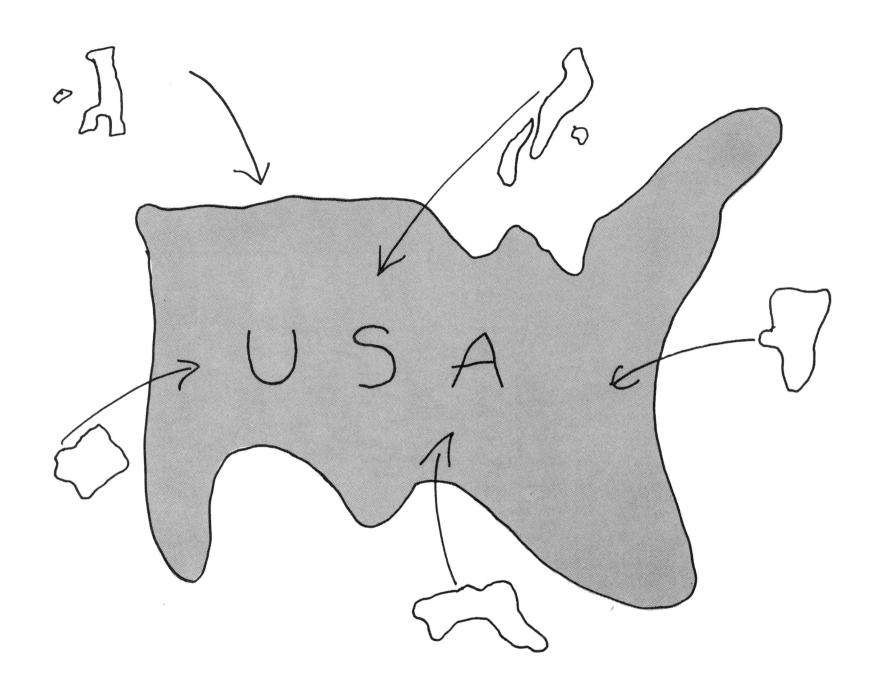

My family is from Vietnam.

In America, almost everybody's family came from another country at one time or another.

Families come to America in many different ways.

We came on a plane.

We came on a boat.

We took a really big train.

We drove over the mountains.

It took a long time to
get to America.

50

How did your family come to America?

Kids usually have lots of thoughts and questions about the country where they used to live.

Will we ever go back to visit?

Will I get to see my friends again?

I wonder who lives in our old house?

What thoughts and questions do you have about the country where you used to live?

Kids also have lots of questions about living in America.

Will I get to have my own room?

Where will we live?

Will we have a car?

What will my new school be like?

What are some of your questions about living in America?

Moving to a new country can feel strange and confusing.

You have to get used to a new house or apartment, a new school, a new teacher, and new friends.

You may have to get used to a new language and a whole different way of doing things.

Kids usually have lots of thoughts and feelings about moving to a new country.

It's hard to move to a whole new country. Sometimes I wish we just stayed where we were. I miss all my friends. Sometimes I feel bad because I don't get everything the teacher says. It's hard to keep up.

Sometimes I get confused because I'm

not really sure which one is my real country.

Even if kids are happy about living in America, they usually miss some things about where they used to live.

What do you miss about the country where you used to live?

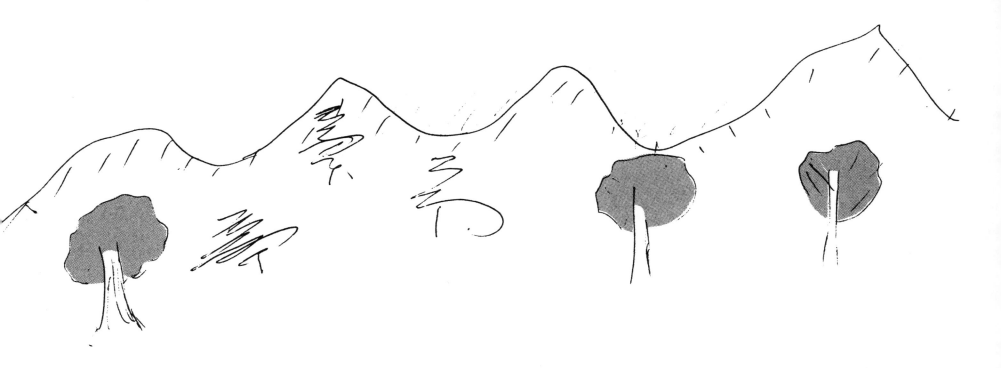

I miss the mountains.

it makes me sad

to see pictures of
Elsalvador on TV. I miss my
friends.

I miss my toys and stuff.

I miss being someplace where everybody knows what you're talking about.

I miss my dog.

I   miss my grandmother. I hope I get to see her again.

I miss our house.

Draw a picture of the place where you used to live.

IN VIET-NAM

Draw a picture of where you live now.

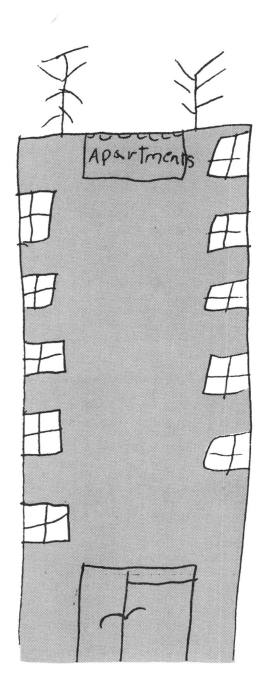

84

85

Most kids also worry about some things when their families move to America.

Will I do okay in school?

Are we safe in our new house?

Will my mom and dad get jobs?

What if I'm no good at baseball?

Will I have friends?

What if nobody likes me?

What if I get all used to living here and have to go somewhere else?

What if everyone has lots and lots of money?

What kinds of things do you worry about?

Countries can be very different from each other.

People may wear different clothes and speak a different language. They may listen to different music and eat different kinds of food.

Can you think of some other things that are different?

There's lots of Food
in the store, and no
long lines - just a short one
where you pay.

You don't have to wear a uniform to School. You can wear whatever you want.

The money looks funny.

Kids play different games.

My dad doesn't have to work on Saturday.

There's more stuff to do.

In America, the cities are really, really big, and there are lots and lots of cars.

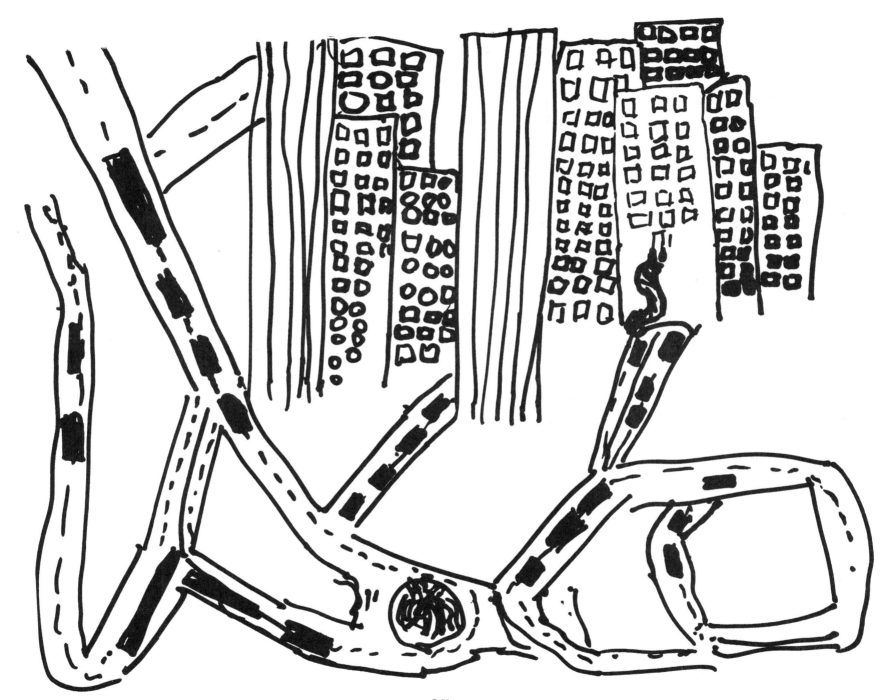

95

In America, kids eat different things for lunch.

Lunch in America

Lunch in Japan

In the U.S. we only have 5 days of school aweek. In Indonesia you had school on saturday, So we had 6 days of school aweek. It's better to have 5 days, because you need rest. I like having 2 days off!

Indonesia

Sun	Mon	Tue	Wed	Thur	Fri	SAT
	1 school	2 school	3 school	4 school	5 school	6 school
	8 school	9 school	10 school	11 school	12 school	13 school
14	15 school	16 school	17 school	18 school	19 school	20 school
21	22 school	23 school	24 school	25 school	26 school	27 school
28	29 school	30 school	31 school			

100

U. S. A.

Sun	Mon	Tue	Wed	Thur	Fri	Sat
	1 school	2 school	3 school	4 school	5 school	6
7	8 school	9 school	10 school	11 school	12 school	13
14	15 school	16 school	17 school	18 school	19 school	20
21	22 school	23 school	24 school	25 school	26 school	27
28	29 school	30 school	31 school			

In America

people are really big.

America

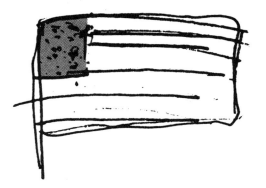

Japanese people are smaller.

Japan

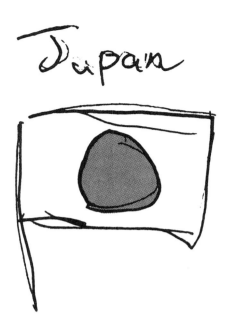

Other things may be similar between two countries:

I still have to do my homework.

My family still lives all together.

I still have my postcard collection.

I still have my teddy bear.

I still play football with my friends,
but here they call it soccer!

Can you think of some other things that are the same?

Some kids already know some English when they come to the United States.

Hi! How are you?

What's your name?

Cheeseburger, Please.

Some come knowing no English at all.

Kids learn to speak English in many ways.

I learned English in school.

My friends teach me English and I'm teaching them Spanish.

English is hard to learn!

I learned English from TV.

When I first came to America, the only word I knew was "Hi".

Some kids help their parents learn English.

I help my mom in the store. She doesn't like to speak English.

I helped my dad fill out some forms for work.

I help my parents read books from school.

I went to the doctor with my grandma.

Most kids like lots of things about living in America.

What things do you like most?

The kids are pretty nice and they like to play.

In America, you can say whatever you want.

I like when it snows.

There are lots of movies

I like my teacher.

We have a TV and a VCR.

What things don't you like about living in America?

It's too hot.

It's too cold.

I don't like taking the bus to school.

There's too much homework.

Everything costs a lot of money.

I don't like getting called
on in class.

Draw a picture of America.

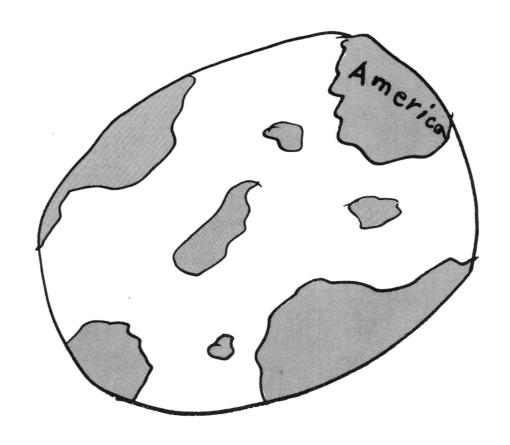

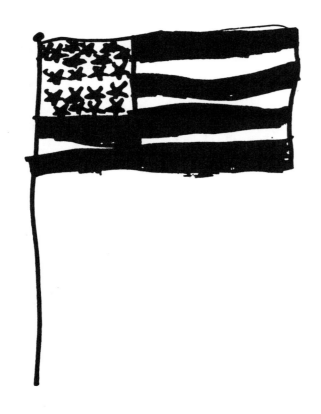

Kids have many thoughts and questions about growing up in America. They also think about the future and have ideas about what they want to do and be.

I want to be a baseball player.

I want to be a doctor.

I want to be a teacher like my mom,

I want to get married, have lots of kids and live in a big house.

I want to be on TV.

I want to help people learn English.

I want to get out of school!

What do you want to do or be when you grow up?

Draw a picture of yourself grown up.

137

139

When I grow up, I want to go back to Czechoslovakia.

Maybe I'll even live there someday.

It's not easy to move to a new country.

When I first came to America I was scared, because I didn't understand anything. Then I made some friends and got used to how things work. I still think a lot about Romania, and I still miss my friends, but I'm glad we moved to America.

If you ask me,

I think

America

is

a pretty

O,K, place.

145

Resources

Agencies and Organizations

American Council on the Teaching of
  Foreign Languages (ACTFL)
6 Executive Plaza
Yonkers, NY 10701-6801

Clearinghouse on Elementary and Early
  Childhood Education
University of Illinois
805 West Pennsylvania Avenue
Urbana, IL 61801

Global Village Catalog of anti-bias products
  for children, educators, and parents
2210 Wilshire Blvd., Box 262
Santa Monica, CA 90403

Modern Lauguage Association (MLA)
10 Astor Place
New York, NY 10003-6981

National Association for the Education and
  Advancement of Cambodian, Laotian and
  Vietnamese Americans (NAFEA)
(415) 885-2743

National Association of Bilingual
  Educators (NABE)
Union Center Plaza
810 First St. NE, 3rd Floor
Washington, DC 20002-4205
(202) 898-1829

National Clearinghouse for Bilingual
  Education
Center for Applied Linguistics
1118 22nd Street N.W.
Washington, DC 20037
(800) 321-NCBE

National Council of Teachers of
  English (NCTE)
111 Kenyon Road
Urbana, IL 61801

Northern New England Teachers of English
  to Speakers of Other Languages C/O ATP
Fiske Annex
Keene State College
Keene, NH 03431

References for Parents and Teachers

Bailey, L., ed. *The Immigrant Experience.* Toronto: Macmillan, 1975.

Crawford, J. *Bilingual Education: History, Politics, Theory, and Practice.* NJ: Crane Publishing Co., 1989.

Gaston, J. *Cultural Awareness Teaching Techniques.* Brattleboro, VT: Pro Lingua Associates, 1984.

Harding E., and Riley, P. *The Bilingual Family: A Handbook for Parents.* New York: Cambridge University Press, 1986.

Kendall, F. E. *Diversity in the Classroom: A Multicultural Approach to the Education of Young Children.* New York: Teachers College Press, 1983.

Kim, Y. Y., and Gudykunst, W., eds. *Cross-Cultural Adaptation: Current Approaches.* New York: Sage Publications, 1988.

Longman Dictionary of American English: A Dictionary for Learners of English. New York: Longman, Inc. 1983.

Nann, R. C., ed. *Uprooting and Surviving.* Reidel, 1982.

Rigg, P., and Allen, V. G. *When They Don't All Speak English: Integrating the ESL Student Into the Regular Classroom.* Urbana, IL: National Council of Teachers of English, 1989.

Troike-Saville, M. *A Guide to Culture in the Classroom.* Washington, D.C National Clearinghouse for Bilingual Education, 1984.

Books for Elementary School Children

Aquino-Mackles, A., King, D. and Bronson, M. *Myself and Others.* New York: Global Perspectives in Education, 1979.

Bjorkman, S., and Baer, E. *This Is the Way We Go to School: A Book About Children Around the World.* New York: Scholastic Inc., 1990.

Caballero, J., and Whordley, D. *Children Around the World.* Atlanta: Humanics Learning, 1984.

Freeman, R. *Immigrant Kids.* New York: E. P. Dutton, 1980.

Friedman, I. *How My Parents Learned to Eat.* Boston: Houghton Mifflin Company, 1984.

Levine, E. *I Hate English.* New York: Scholastic, 1989.

Marsoli, L. A. *Things to Know Before You Move.* Silver LB, 1985.

Milord, S. *Hands Around the World,* Charlotte, VT: Williamson Publishing, 1982.

Rosenberg, M. *Living in Two Worlds.* New York: Lothrop Lee and Shepard Books, 1986.

Rosenberg, M. *Making a New Home in America.* New York: Lothrop Lee and Shepard Books, 1986.

Stanek, M. *We Came From Vietnam.* Nile, IL: Albert Whitman and Co., 1985.

Stanek, M. *I Speak English for My Mom.* Nile, IL: Albert Whitman and Co., 1989.

Surat, M. M. and Mai, V. *Angel Child, Dragon Child.* New York: Scholastic Inc., 1983.

About the Authors

David Fassler, M.D. is a child and adolescent psychiatrist practicing in Burlington, Vermont. A graduate of the Yale University School of Medicine, Dr. Fassler received his training in adult psychiatry at the University of Vermont, and in child psychiatry at the Cambridge Hospital, Harvard Medical School. He is currently a clinical assistant professor and the director of continuing education in the Department of Psychiatry at the University of Vermont, and an instructor in psychiatry at Cambridge Hospital, Harvard Medical School. He is also a co-author of a series of children's books dealing with family transitions and health-related issues. Dr. Fassler also serves as the director of child and adolescent psychiatry for Choate Health Systems in Woburn, Massachusetts, and as medical director of the Center for Child and Family Development at New England Memorial Hospital in Stoneham, Massachusetts.

Kimberly Danforth, M.A. is an instructor in English as a second language in Burlington, Vermont and coordinator of special projects in the Department of Psychiatry at the University of Vermont. A graduate of the Sorbonne, France, UVM, and the University of Massachusetts at Amherst, Ms. Danforth is also a free-lance writer specializing in multicultural issues.